Oxford University Press, Walton Street, Oxford OX2 6DP

Oxford New York Toronto
Delhi Bombay Calcutta Madras Karachi
Petaling Jaya Singapore Hong Kong Tokyo
Nairobi Dar es Salaam Cape Town
Melbourne Auckland

and associated companies in
Beirut Berlin Ibadan Nicosia

Oxford is a trade mark of Oxford University Press

British Library Cataloguing in Publication Data
Haas, Rick de
Wild goose chase.
I. Title II. Gat in de zandbak. *English*
839.3'1364[J] PZ7
ISBN 0-19-279850-2

Typeset by Cotswold Graphics, Stroud, Gloucestershire

Printed in Belgium ⊠

WILD GOOSE CHASE

RICK DE HAAS

English version by Rachel Anderson

Oxford University Press

Oxford Toronto Melbourne

'You'll just play here quietly, won't you?' my mum says to me. She wants to pop down to the shops. 'I shan't be gone long,' she says.

'Yes, mum.'

'Now be a good boy, won't you? Don't do anything silly.'

'No, mum.'

'Or dangerous.'

'No, mum.'

'And keep an eye on Bruno for me. Don't let him run off.'

'Yes, mum. Bye, mum.'

Off she goes. And I can get on with my digging. My friend says if you keep digging long enough you get to Australia.

Yikes! What's this I've found?

A door! Right at the bottom of my sandpit. And it's got a handle. Turn the handle carefully. Open, Sesame. And there's a little entrance hall. How odd. I wonder if it's been there long?

And a passage. Better follow it, find out where it goes.

First I'll put some useful things in my basket. A packet of biscuits. My swimming goggles. You never know, they might come in handy.

'Bruno! 'Come on boy. Walkies time!'

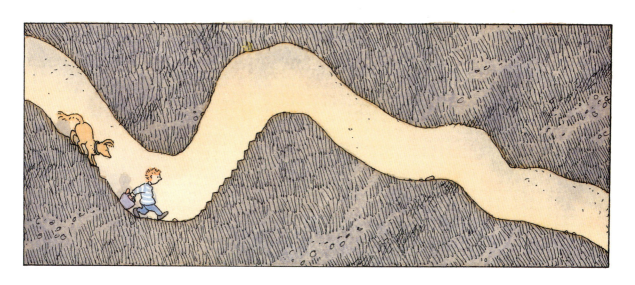

Along a bit. Down a bit. Up a bit. Down again. Keep going.

Whew! I smell fresh air at last. Glad I'm not a mole. Aha, daylight above, too.

'Bruno, I told you to keep up. Or mum'll be furious.'

Well I never, there's someone waiting for us.

'Good morning, er, sir.' If it is a sir. Looks more like a rat or a vole. Peculiaarrr.

'You're late!'

Late? How could I be? I didn't even know I was coming.

'Get in quickly. And no dogs in the car. Madam can't abide dogs, you know that perfectly well.'

Do I? Oh dear, poor Bruno. He'll have to run behind.

'Good dog, Bruno. You must try to keep up. Run as fast as you can or you'll get left behind, and you'll never find your way out of these woods alone.'

Quickly, Bruno! Please hurry!

Bruno bounds in through the gates. But the guards have
seen him. 'No dogs upstairs. Or she'll have a fit.'

Poor Bruno, having to wait downstairs, and tied up too. They're really very rude round here. Don't let dogs in, shove visitors about. Never say please. I'd better show them a few good manners.

'Good day, your ladyship, er, your highness.'

'Aha, so there you are, young man. And high time too. I can't stand any slackness, you know, especially when you're on the job.'

'No, ma'am.'

What job is she on about? A job? For me?

'You've got your things?'

'Eer.' Which things can she mean? 'Yes, your ladyship. I've brought one or two biscuits, and my sandbucket, and of course my swimming goggles.'

'Good. Very well. It's late now. Far too late to set out after that treasure. So you'll just have to make an early start tomorrow. My guards will show you to your room.'

'But Bruno! My dog!'

'I can't abide dogs. You know that perfectly well. Good-night.'

What a night. So long. And I hardly slept a wink. I thought I'd try and get out of here, then I found they've locked me in.

Poor Bruno. I hope he's O.K. I bet he's missing me. I wonder if they gave him any supper. They didn't give *me* any. Lucky I had those biscuits with me.

'Psst. Psst.'

What's that? It's one of those creatures again, tapping at the door.

'Yes? What is it?'

'Psst. Wake up, you. Time to set off for the mixer-monster mountain. Follow me. And *hurry*!'

'But my dog. I can't leave him here.'

'That canine is our hostage. To make sure you come back with the treasure. Off with you now, and be quick about it.'

'But where have I got to go to?'

'You must row downstream till you can't row any more. You'll hear it soon enough.'

I've rowed and rowed just like he said, but I haven't got anywhere. I'm so tired. So hungry. No biscuits left. Nothing to drink.

Owww! What's that? Something's got me. Owwch. In the neck.

Help! I'm being whizzed through the air on a boathook.
And ooh, it's dark in here! Wherever am I now?

'Ah, there you are, duckie!'

Oooooeerr. Is this the terrible mixer-monster?

'Feeling better now, are we, duckie? You'll be safe with me.'

'Safe? You mean, you're not the monster?'

'Dearie me, no. Now come up on deck and we'll soon be home.'

'Home?'

'To my home. I've rescued dozens of little boys like you.'

'Rescued?'

'You didn't think that dreadful old woman would *really* let
you go once you'd found her the treasure, did you, duckie?'

'Well, er, I didn't really think.'

Come and have some nice tea at my palace.'

'Come upstairs, and I'll give you a peek at the monster's mountain.'

Ooooh, scarreee. Do I *really* want to have to go there?

'Of course, duckie, you mustn't go on your own. It wouldn't be safe. But the boy will take you. He knows the way.'

'The boy?'

'One of the lads I rescued. I couldn't send him home. He hadn't got one to go to.'

'Now come on and eat up. Build up your strength. Have another éclair, won't you?'

Nothing but cream cakes and more cream cakes. What a diet. No wonder she's so porky. Goodness, what on earth's she got hold of here? Looks like a couple of dead ducks.

'Here's your disguises, boys. Slip them on. That's the way.'

I feel such a silly goose.

'My! That is simply splendid, my dears. You look just like the real thing. But do you *have* to keep your goggles on, duckie? Oh well, never mind, they hardly show.'

Shall I tell her I don't like water in my eyes when I'm swimming? No, better not. The boy will think I'm a coward.

'And don't forget your waterproof backpacks, boys. They've got your emergency disguises. Though I hope you won't be needing them. Off you waddle then, my lovelies.'

'I say, are you *sure* you know the way?'
'Oink.'

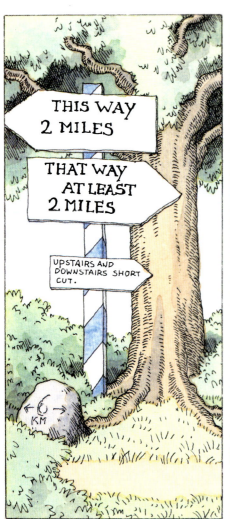

Land at last. Now where do we go?

'It's this way, oink.'

'No, it's not. It's that way. I'm sure it must be.'

'Come on. I've got the map so I must be right. It's your stupid goggles. You can't see anything through them.'

This is no time to argue with him.

'See! Here we are. This must be it. Oink.'

He's right. And there's all the little piggies that went to market and wouldn't stay at home. I'm scared. Oink.

'Oink. What's that *terrible* noise?'

'And what's that *awful* smell?'

'Sounds like a mixer-monster mixing to me.'

'Smells like it, too.'

Yes! It's the dreaded mixer-monster at work. BEWARE!

'Oink. Look, there's the treasure!'

'Can't see it.'

'That's because your goggles are getting misted up. Look, oink. Up there. Under the tea-towel.'

'Sniff-sniffle. Snuff-snuffle! I smell tasty goose-fat. I smell delicious trouble. Anybody there? Who's there?'

'Quick, grab the treasure before our goose is cooked.'

Keeerrump-Phplat! The mixer-monster's met her match!

Woweee! We're out of the frying pan and into the lake.
Beware of falling geese.

Another close shave.

'I say there, are you all right, brother goose? You seem a bit water-logged.'

'So I've lost my goggles and we've both lost the treasure. And we've still got to find Bruno.'

'This way. Yes, this is definitely the place I last saw him.'

'Well there's no dog here now.'

'Oh, poor Bruno. I hope he's all right.'

'Quickly then into our emergency disguises and we'll try and slip into the palace.'

'Bruno. Bruno. Where are you? Can you hear me? I've come to fetch you.'

'Aaah, dear Bruno. Soon have you free. There now. It's walkies time again.'

'Which way? This way?'

'Or that-a-way?'

'Oh, well done! Bruno
knows the way.
Good dog.'

'And here's the way out. Bye.
See you again some day. In we go,
come on Bruno.'

'Hello, mum. Hello, dad. I'm back.'

'Ah, there you are, Oliver.'

'I say, did you know about this amazing tunnel I found? And right at the end of it I met this lady and I had to spend the night in her palace. And then me and another boy got disguised as geese.'

'Yes, dear. And you're just in time for tea. Go and wash your hands. I've got some lovely cream cakes.'

'D'you know, Bruno, I don't think she's listening to a word I'm saying.'

'You didn't let Bruno out of the garden, did you? I couldn't see him anywhere.'

'No, mum. He's been with me all the time. Well, nearly all the time, haven't you, Bruno?'

'Nrrr.'